Get Mapping!

...es of Maps

Melanie Waldron

Raintree is an imprint of Capstone Global Library Limited, a company incorporated in England and Wales having its registered office at 7 Pilgrim Street, London, EC4V 6LB – Registered company number: 6695582

To contact Raintree please phone 0845 6044371, fax + 44 (0) 1865 312263, or email myorders@ raintreepublishers.co.uk. Customers from outside the UK please telephone +44 1865 312262.

Text © Capstone Global Library Limited 2013
First published in hardback in 2013
First published in paperback in 2014
The moral rights of the proprietor have been asserted.

Edited by Nancy Dickmann and Abby Colich
Designed by Victoria Allen
Original illustrations © 2013
Illustrated by HL Studios
Picture research by Ruth Blair
Originated by Capstone Global Library Limited
Printed and bound in China by CTPS

ISBN 978 1 406 24923 1 (hardback)
16 15 14 13 12
10 9 8 7 6 5 4 3 2 1

ISBN 978 1 406 24930 9 (paperback)
17 16 15
10 9 8 7 6 5 4 3 2

British Library Cataloguing in Publication Data
Waldron, Melanie.
Types of maps. -- (Let's get mapping!)
912-dc23
A full catalogue record for this book is available from the British Library.

Acknowledgements

We would like to thank the following for permission to reproduce photographs: Alamy: pp. 6 (© fStop), 10 (© M Itani), 19 (© imagebroker); ©ATCO: p. 11; iStockphoto: p. 21 (© Emrah Turudu); Shutterstock: pp. 5 (© Noel Powell, Schaumburg), 7 (© Alfonso de Tomas), 13 (© djgis), 14 (© Tyler Olson), 20 (© algabafoto), 22 (© Pichugin Dmitry); Superstock: pp. 4 (© Cultura Limited), 25 (© Photononstop), 26 (© Fotosearch); Wellcome Library, London: p. 17.

Cover photograph of a GPS over a paper map is reproduced with permission from Shutterstock (© Pincasso).

Background images and design features reproduced with permission from Shutterstock.

Every effort has been made to contact copyright holders of material reproduced in this book. Any omissions will be rectified in subsequent printings if notice is given to the publisher.

Contents

Some words appear in the text in bold, **like this**. You can find out what they mean by looking in the glossary.

What is a map?

When you think of a map, you might think of a flat piece of paper. It will show some **symbols**. These are little pictures or shapes that represent things in real life. For example, a white square with a red cross on it might represent a hospital.

A map is a way of showing information about the land. There are many different types of maps that can show different types of information. There could be many maps of one area, each one showing different information.

Skiers use **piste maps** to find the correct route down a mountain. This can stop them getting lost or skiing off a steep cliff!

What are maps for?

Maps help people travel around and find places. They can be used to learn about different places and how people live there. Maps can also be used to help us explain things, for example, the weather.

Sailors use maps of the sea floor to avoid hitting rocks and sandbanks under the water.

PAPERLESS MAPS

Today, many people use digital maps. These are maps that you can see on a screen, such as a computer or mobile phone. There are millions of online maps available on the internet.

Round Earth, flat map

Earth is not flat! Our planet is a **sphere,** like a ball. The most accurate map of Earth is called a **globe**. It can spin round so you can see where all the countries are. A globe really helps us to see the position of each country and **continent** on Earth.

Although globes are very useful, there are some problems with using them. They are difficult to carry around and store. They can't be used inside books, and they usually cost a lot more than flat paper maps.

Globes can show us where countries, continents, and oceans are located on Earth.

Flattened Earth

Flat paper maps can be carried around or used inside books and newspapers. When we use flat maps, we have to imagine that Earth has been squashed flat. **Cartographers**, people who make maps, have clever ways to do this.

A flat map uses something called a **projection** to make it flat. There are different kinds of projections. Each one squashes Earth in a different way.

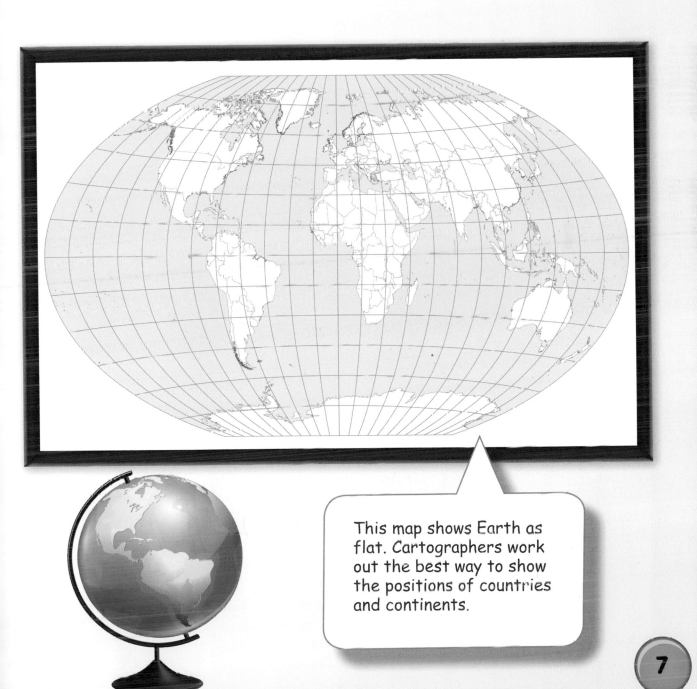

This map shows Earth as flat. Cartographers work out the best way to show the positions of countries and continents.

Political and physical maps

Political maps show areas of land and their **borders**. Borders are imaginary lines that separate things. International borders separate countries. Different counties, regions, or states inside countries have borders to separate them.

Many borders are simply lines on a map. Sometimes a **natural feature** such as a river can be a border. Often, there is nothing in real life to show where borders are.

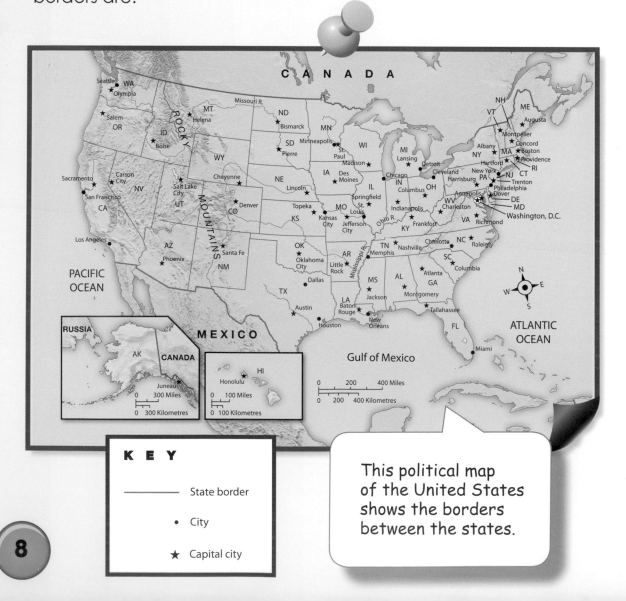

This political map of the United States shows the borders between the states.

KEY

———— State border

• City

★ Capital city

Physical maps

Maps that show the shape of the land are called **physical maps**. They also show natural features such as rivers and lakes. They show areas that are flat and areas that are hilly or mountainous. Many physical maps also show the borders between countries, and some show buildings and roads.

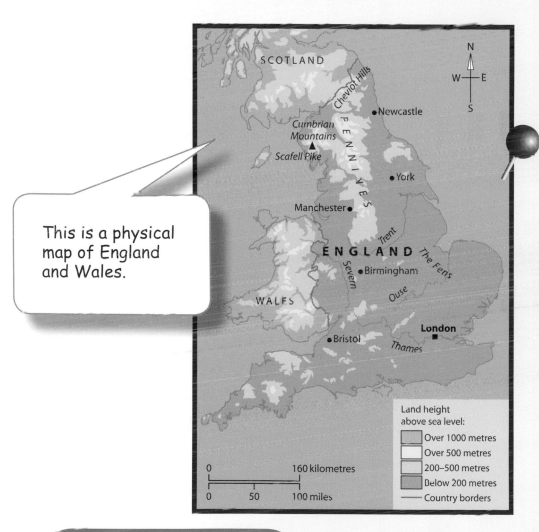

This is a physical map of England and Wales.

Land height above sea level:

- Over 1000 metres
- Over 500 metres
- 200–500 metres
- Below 200 metres
- —— Country borders

DIVIDING PEOPLE

Some of the international borders in Africa were created by European governments in the 1800s. The border between Kenya and Tanzania was created in 1890. This split up an area called Maasailand, where the Maasai people had lived together for thousands of years.

Transport maps

Many countries have lots of roads. Most people need road maps to help them drive around the country. Detailed road maps have almost all roads marked on them. They also show cities, towns, and villages.

Road maps need to show twists and turns in the roads. All the roads need to follow the same direction as in real life. This is to help drivers work out where they are and where they need to go.

On this road map, motorways are blue, main roads are green, and other roads are orange. Narrow, winding roads are grey.

Railways

Countries with railways need maps to help people plan their train journeys. Railway maps don't need to show the twists and turns of the railway lines. This means that railway maps can sometimes look very different from the real-life railway lines.

This map shows some train routes for Scotland and England. It shows the railway lines as very straight and the stations evenly spaced out.

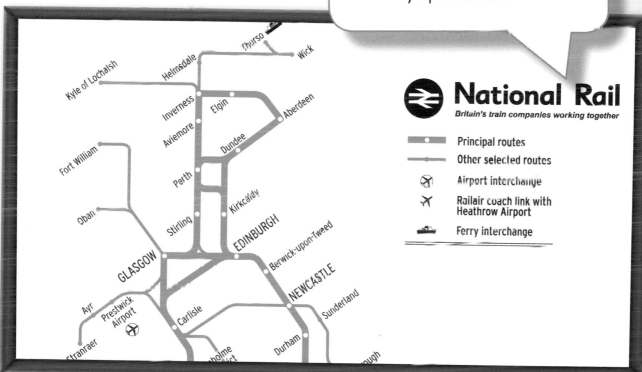

National Rail
Britain's train companies working together

Principal routes
Other selected routes
Airport interchange
Railair coach link with Heathrow Airport
Ferry interchange

Thurso
Wick
Kyle of Lochalsh
Helmsdale
Inverness
Elgin
Aberdeen
Aviemore
Dundee
Fort William
Perth
Oban
Kirkcaldy
Stirling
EDINBURGH
Berwick-upon-Tweed
GLASGOW
NEWCASTLE
Ayr
Prestwick Airport
Carlisle
Sunderland
Stranraer
Durham

SATNAV

Satnav is short for "satellite navigation". Many modern cars have satnav systems. These show digital maps on a small screen and tell the driver where to go. Many drivers no longer use paper road maps.

Weather and topography

Weather maps are useful for showing us what the weather in our area is like. **Weather forecast** maps show us what the weather might be like over the next few days. Weather maps show very little information about what is on the land. They usually just show some towns and cities to help us know which area we are looking at.

This weather forecast map shows what the weather will be like in Europe and North Africa.

CHANGING MAPS

Weather maps are always changing! They use different symbols to show us how the weather is changing and what type of weather we should expect. Online maps can be updated several times a day as weather forecasters update their forecasts.

Land details

Topographical maps show huge amounts of detail about the land's surface. They usually have **contour lines** to tell us how high the land is, and how steep or flat it is. A contour line runs along all the land at the same height. Contour lines spaced far apart tell us that the land is quite flat. Contour lines packed closely together tell us that the land is very steep.

Topographical maps give us very detailed information about the shape of the land.

Land use and resources

Making maps of the way the land is used can help us to understand many things about an area. A land-use map of Nepal, a mountainous country, would show that large areas are used for tourism and conservation.

Land-use maps can use symbols to show different types of land use. They can also use different colours to represent different land uses. There are lots of different land uses, including farming, housing, and transport.

A land-use map of the United States will show that huge areas are used for growing cereal crops.

Mapping resources

Resource maps can show us the important resources of an area, such as coal, oil, and diamonds. People use maps to work out the best places to explore for these things.

Resource maps can also include things like wind. Energy can be captured using windmills, so it is useful to know where windy places are.

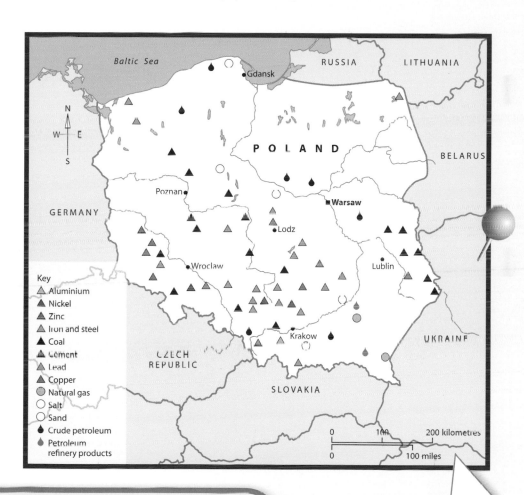

Key
△ Aluminium
▲ Nickel
▲ Zinc
△ Iron and steel
▲ Coal
▲ Cement
△ Lead
▲ Copper
⦿ Natural gas
◯ Salt
◯ Sand
⬥ Crude petroleum
⬥ Petroleum refinery products

This is a resource map of Poland. It shows where some valuable resources can be found.

PRECIOUS WATER

Fresh water is a very precious resource in many areas of the world. It is becoming more important to map water – even underground water resources – so that it can be used wisely and protected from pollution.

Statistical maps

Many maps show information about countries and the people living there. Statistical maps show **statistics**. Statistics are numbers. All kinds of numbers can be represented on a map.

Statistical maps can show information in different ways. Different sizes of symbols could show different numbers of things. For example, a small circle could show all villages with fewer than 1,000 people. A large circle could show cities with over 1,000,000 people.

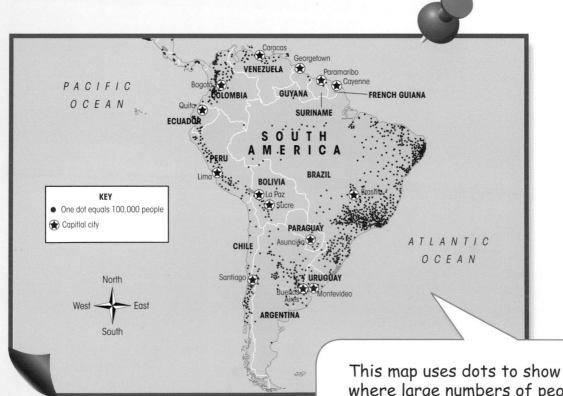

KEY
● One dot equals 100,000 people
⭐ Capitlal city

This map uses dots to show where large numbers of people live in South America. This is more useful than a table of figures, as you can see at a glance where the highest populations are.

Different statistics

A world map could show the average temperature for each country. A map of a country could show the percentage of people aged over 60 in each city. A map of a town could show the number of people living in each house.

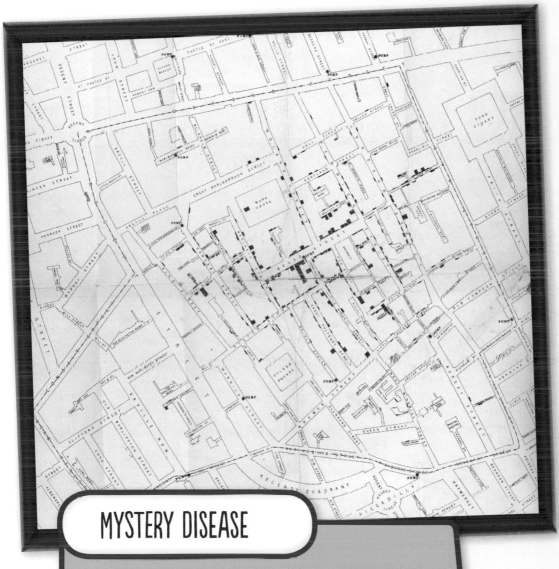

MYSTERY DISEASE

John Snow was a doctor, living in London in the 1800s. He marked on this map where people with a disease called **cholera** lived. He used the map to work out where the cholera was coming from – a nearby water pump. The pump handle was removed, and the cholera cases decreased.

Tourist maps and town maps

Maps of your local area show small areas of land. They can show lots of detail about the land, far more detail than a world map or country map could show. These maps are called large-scale maps. Maps that show much less detail, but cover a much larger area, are called small-scale maps.

Large-scale maps of a town or city can be really useful. They can include street names to help us find places and addresses. They can use symbols to show important buildings. They can also show where bus stops and bus routes are.

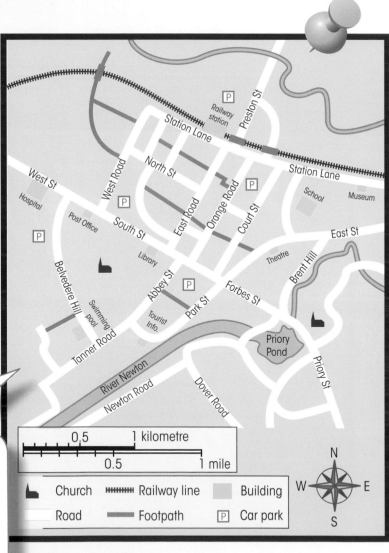

This is a large-scale map of a town centre. Some of the streets are named and some locations have symbols.

18

Pictorial maps

Some areas that have lots of visiting tourists have special tourist maps. These show the things that might be interesting for tourists – museums, restaurants, and hotels, for example. Some towns or parks use **pictorial maps**. These maps show tiny drawings of the buildings and attractions. Pictorial maps are fun to look at, and make it easier for tourists to find things.

This pictorial map shows the city centre of Elche, Spain. There are little drawings of some of the buildings.

Historical maps, modern maps

People have been making and using maps for hundreds of years. Many of the first maps were made by explorers who were sailing to new places. Often, they made their maps from sketches of the areas they explored.

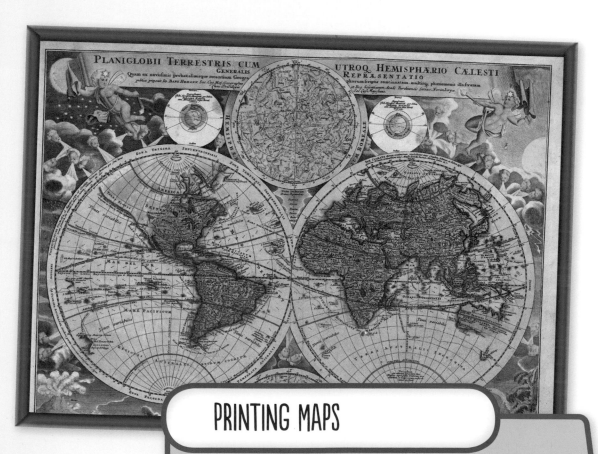

PRINTING MAPS

Until the 1400s, maps had to be hand-drawn and copied by hand. This made them very rare and also very expensive. During the 1400s, printing machines were invented. This meant that copies of maps could be made, and more people could own them.

Modern maps

Today, most maps are made using **aerial photographs** and **satellite images**. Aerial photographs are taken by cameras fitted to aeroplanes. Satellites can take very detailed photographs of Earth's surface.

Surveyors help cartographers by checking the land at ground level. They make sure that the aerial photographs and satellite images are accurate. They also provide information that cartographers can't tell from photographs, for example, street names and building types.

Many modern maps are digital, and are displayed on screens instead of being printed on paper.

Same place, different map

In this book, you have seen that there are many different kinds of maps. They all contain different information and they are all used for slightly different purposes. This means that any one area could have lots of different maps, all showing different things.

A map of this area could show that very few people live here, or how the land is used.

Mixing information

Sometimes it is useful to see a mix of different kinds of information on a map. This means that we can try to explain patterns. For example, a map showing where people live around the world would show areas of high and low population. If you added information about the world's weather to this map, you would see that there are very few people where the weather is usually very cold or very hot and dry.

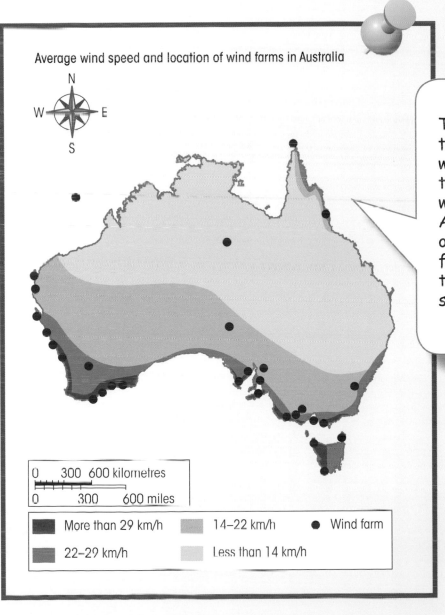

Average wind speed and location of wind farms in Australia

This map shows the location of wind farms, and the average wind speeds, in Australia. Most of the wind farms are where the average wind speed is highest.

0   300 600 kilometres

0   300   600 miles

More than 29 km/h   14–22 km/h   ● Wind farm

22–29 km/h   Less than 14 km/h

Reading maps

Reading a map is a very useful skill. It can help you travel around and find places. If you can read a map, you can also find out some really useful information about places.

> If you had to follow the trail on this map, it would be helpful if you knew how to read the map!

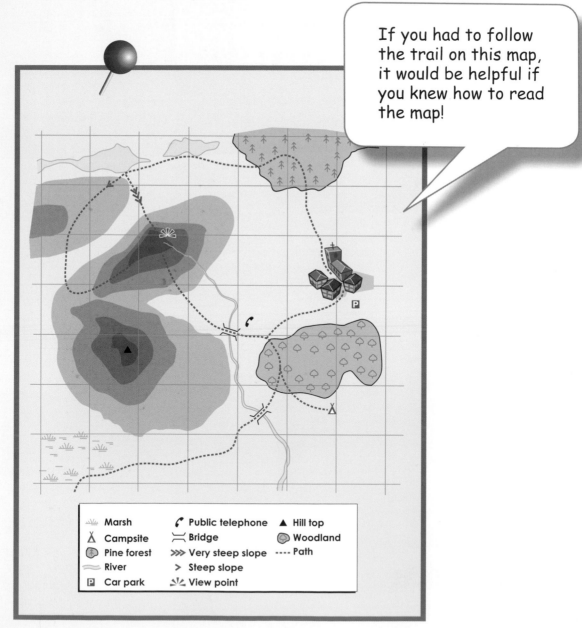

Marsh	✆ Public telephone	▲ Hill top
⋀ Campsite	⋈ Bridge	Woodland
Pine forest	⋙ Very steep slope	---- Path
River	> Steep slope	
P Car park	View point	

Important map-reading skills

Whatever type of map you are looking at, some basic skills are important. Firstly, always check the map's title. Then you will know what the map is trying to show you.

Most maps have a **compass rose** printed on them, showing which way is North, South, East, and West on the map. Use a compass to make sure you have the map turned the right way round, so it matches North, South, East, and West in real life.

To help you work out distances in real life, use the **scale bar** on the map. This is a line or bar with numbers printed on it. If you measure the distance you want to know about and then hold this against the scale bar, you can work out the distance.

Street maps can help you to walk around places without getting lost.

Space maps

There are some maps that don't show any part of Earth at all – maps of space! The first maps of the Moon were made in the 1960s, to see if it would be possible to land a spaceship on it. NASA, the US space agency, has also made maps of Mars, Mercury, Venus, and the moons of Jupiter and Saturn.

The Hubble Space Telescope was launched in 1990. It sends amazing images of space back to Earth.

Mapping the sky

Maps of the night sky, as seen from Earth, have been used for hundreds of years. Sailors used them to help them sail their ships in the right direction. Night sky maps show the planets that are near Earth. They also show stars that are incredibly far away.

Maps of the night sky are different for different locations around the world. The night sky also changes as Earth turns. This means that you must make sure you are looking at the correct night sky map for your area. Once you have the correct map, you can start to name the stars and planets you can see.

Night sky maps show the stars and planets that are visible from Earth.

NORTH

CASSIOPEIA

CEPHEUS

URSA MINOR

THE PLOUGH
(PART OF URSA MAJOR)

DRACO

DELPHINUS

CYGNUS

HERCULES

BOOTES

EAST

WEST

LYRA

CORONA BOREALIS

AQUILA

SERPENS CAPUT

LIBRA

SERPENS CAUDA

OPHIUCHUS

SAGITTARIUS

SCORPIUS

SOUTH

Get mapping!

Look at these three maps. They show the same area, but they show different information about the area.

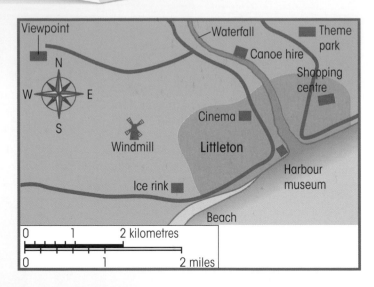

A

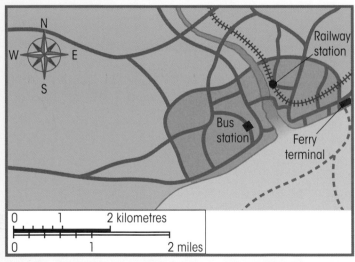

B

C

Land	Marshy area	Contour line
Built-up area	Cliffs	
Beach	River	

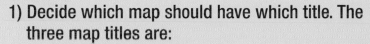

1) Decide which map should have which title. The three map titles are:

- Littleton Area Transport Networks and Terminals
- Littleton Area Tourist Features
- Littleton Area Topography

2) Which map would you use if you were planning a long walk in the countryside?

3) Which map would you send to friends who were planning to visit the town?

4) Which map would be useful for a business that wanted to transport its goods?

5) Imagine you wanted to add more information to one of the maps. For example, you could add some weather information. Choose the map you think would be the best one to use. You could trace it and add weather information to it. Why did you choose that map? Who might want to know about the weather? Would they have chosen the same map as you?

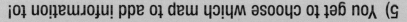

Glossary

aerial photograph photograph taken from high above Earth's surface, usually from an aeroplane

border imaginary line that separates different countries, or different regions inside a country

cartographer person who makes maps

cholera dangerous infectious disease that causes stomach cramps and sickness

compass rose drawing with four points, showing where North, South, East, and West are on a map

continent one of Earth's seven major areas of land: North America, South America, Europe, Africa, Asia, Australasia, and Antarctica

contour line line that follows all the land at a certain height above sea level

globe round ball with a map of Earth on it

natural feature something on Earth's surface that has been created by nature, for example a mountain

physical map map that shows the shape of the land and its natural features

pictorial map map that has tiny drawings of the features it wants to show; often used in popular tourist places

piste map map of the ski runs and ski lifts in a ski area

political map map that shows countries and their borders, and often capital cities

projection way of displaying an image on a screen or flat area

resource something that is of value to humans that Earth can provide

satellite image picture, like a photograph, that a satellite can take of Earth from space

scale bar bar or line on a map which shows you how far a distance on the map represents in real life

sphere solid, round object

statistic number that gives information about something

symbol object or a picture that represents something

weather forecast weather that is likely to happen in a place in the near future

Find out more

There is a whole world of maps and mapping waiting to be discovered! Try looking at some other books and some websites to start you off.

Books

Introducing Maps (Maps and Mapping Skills), Meg and Jack Gillett (Wayland, 2010)

Map Types, Kate Torpie (Crabtree Publishing, 2008)

The Atlas of Space, J. Challoner (Franklin Watts, 2008)

Types of Maps (Ways to Find Your Way), Kay Jackson (Capstone Press, 2008)

Websites

www.bbc.co.uk/weather
This is the BBC's weather home page. You can see weather maps and forecasts for the UK. You can type in the postcode for your area and get a more detailed forecast.

mapzone.ordnancesurvey.co.uk/mapzone/index.html
This is an interactive website all about maps and mapping, with homework help, maps, photos, and games. The teaching resources section includes lots of useful sheets about map skills.

www.oxfam.org.uk/education/resources/mapping_our_world/ mapping_our_world/l/home/index.htm
On this website, you will find puzzles and games as well as some different kinds of maps.

www.worldmapper.org/index.html
This website has lots of different maps of the world. The information is shown in an unusual way!

Index